Sight

First published in the U.S. in 1994 by Carolrhoda Books, Inc.
c/o The Lerner Group
241 First Avenue North, Minneapolis, Minnesota 55401

Copyright © 1993 Wayland (Publishers) Ltd., Hove, East Sussex
First published 1993 Wayland (Publishers) Ltd.

Library of Congress Cataloging-in-Publication Data

Suhr, Mandy.
  Sight / written by Mandy Suhr ; illustrated by Mike Gordon.
     p.   cm. – (I'm alive)
  Originally published: Wayland Publishers, 1993.
  ISBN 0-87614-834-8
  1. Vision–Juvenile literature. [1. Vision. 2. Senses and
sensation.] I. Gordon, Mike, ill. II. Title. III. Series: Suhr, Mandy.
I'm alive.
QP475.7.S84 1994   93-44193
612.8′4–dc20   CIP
                                                          AC

Printed in Italy by Rotolito Lombarda S.p.A., Milan
Bound in the United States of America

1 2 3 4 5 6 – P/OS – 99 98 97 96 95 94

Sight

written by Mandy Suhr
illustrated by Mike Gordon

Carolrhoda Books, Inc.
Minneapolis

Look around you. What can you see?

How many different colors
can you see?

How many different shapes
can you see?

You can see things that are very close.

You can see things that are far away.

You see things that make
you feel happy.

TOOT,
TOOT!

You see things that make you feel sad.

7

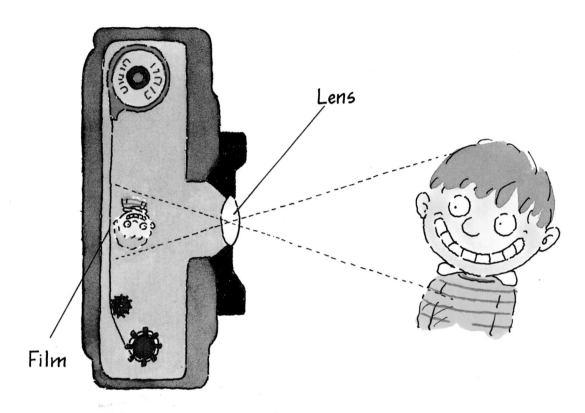

Lens

Film

You use your eyes to see. Your eye is
a little like a camera. It works by
letting light in from the world
outside. Inside your eye is a lens,
like the one inside a camera.

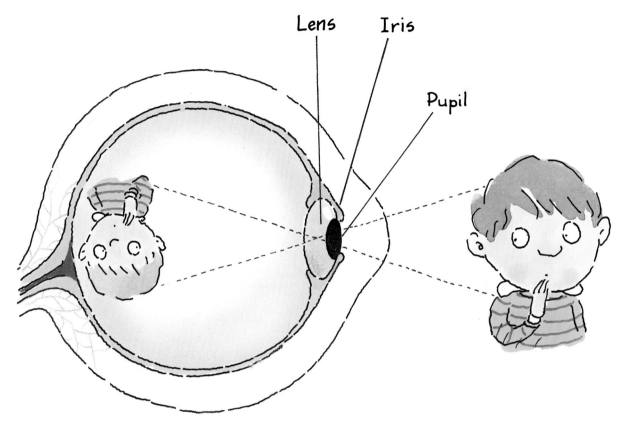

Lens Iris

Pupil

The lens focuses the light to make a tiny picture at the back of your eye. This picture is upside down, just like in the camera. Your brain turns it right side up for you.

At the back of your eyes are light detectors. They send messages to your brain along pathways called nerves.

These messages tell your brain what your eyes are seeing.

The light goes into your eye through a hole called a pupil. This is the black part of your eye.

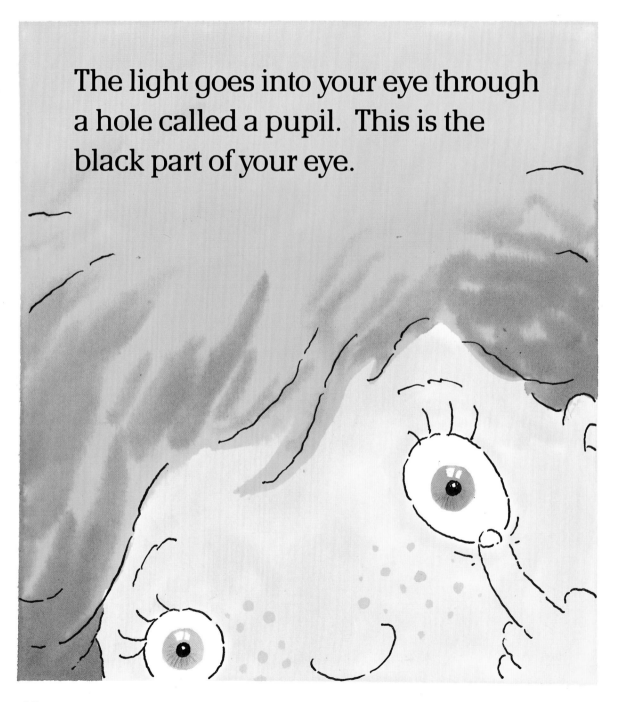

The colored part of your eye is called the iris.

This part is stretchy and makes the pupil bigger when it is dark...

and smaller when it is light, so just the right amount of light gets in.

Your eyes are protected by eyelids and eyelashes. They keep out dust and dirt.

There are tiny holes at the inside corner of each eye. Salty water called tears comes from these holes to wash your eyes and keep them clean.

Some things are so small you
can only see them well through a
magnifying glass. This makes
them look bigger.

Some things are so small they can't
be seen at all by your eyes alone.
But you might be able to see them
if you look through a microscope.

Being able to see is very useful. It can stop you from hurting yourself.

It can also help you
stop other people from
being hurt.

Some people's eyes don't work well.
They need help to see clearly, so
they wear glasses.

Glasses make things look clearer.
The lenses in glasses help the lenses
in your eyes focus.

Some people can't see at all.
They have to use their other
senses instead.

This man uses a cane to help him
get around.

Some blind people have dogs that are specially trained to help them.

Both of your eyes point forward. You have to turn your head to see all around you.

But some animals, like these rabbits, have an eye on each side of their head. They can see all around them without turning their head.

Some animals can see very well, even from a long way off. This eagle has very good eyesight, which helps it to catch its food.

You can see a long way just by using your eyes. But if you look through a telescope, you can see even farther! Try this for yourself and see how far you can see.

A note to adults

"I'm Alive" is a series of books designed especially for preschoolers and beginning readers. These books look at how the human body works and develops. They compare the human body to plants, animals, and objects that are already familiar to children.

Here are some activities that use what kids already know to learn more about their sense of sight.

Activities

1. Make your own magnifying lens. Spread a piece of clear plastic wrap over a roll of tape. Place the roll of tape over the words in this book and look through the plastic at the letters. Do they look any different? Now pour a few drops of water on the plastic. Look at the words through the plastic again. What happens to the letters this time?

2. Go on a nature walk with a magnifying glass. Use the glass to get a close-up look at such things as tree bark, flowers, insects, and even dirt. Don't forget that you are a part of nature, too. Look at your own skin through the magnifying glass.

3. Do you have eyes on the sides of your head? Look straight ahead at a point in the distance. Take a small bright-colored object, such as a red ball, and hold it at your eye level behind your head. Slowly bring the object around the side of your head, keeping the object at eye level. Continue to look at the point in the distance, and don't turn your head. How soon can you see the color of the object? How soon can you see what the object is? The ability to see objects on either side of you while looking straight ahead is called peripheral vision.

4. Try this experiment with a friend. Dim the lights in the room. Wait a minute or two to let your eyes get used to the low light. Look at the size of your friend's pupils–the black circles in the center of his or her eyes. Then point a flashlight at your friend's face and turn it on. (Tell your friend not to look directly at the light.) Watch what happens to the pupils. You can also do this experiment alone using a mirror.

Titles in This Series

How I Breathe

I Am Growing

I Can Move

When I Eat

Sight

Touch

Smell

Taste

Hearing